autobiography of my hungers

LIVING OUT

Gay and Lesbian Autobiographies

David Bergman, Joan Larkin, and Raphael Kadushin
SERIES EDITORS

rigoberto gonzález

autobiography of my hungers

The University of Wisconsin Press

The University of Wisconsin Press
1930 Monroe Street, 3rd Floor
Madison, Wisconsin 53711-2059
uwpress.wisc.edu

3 Henrietta Street
London WC2E 8LU, England
eurospanbookstore.com

Printed in the United States of America

Library of Congress Cataloging-in-Publication Data

González, Rigoberto.
Autobiography of my hungers / Rigoberto González.
p.   cm.—(Living out: gay and lesbian autobiographies)
ISBN 978-0-299-29250-8 (cloth: alk. paper)
ISBN 978-0-299-29253-9 (e-book)
1. González, Rigoberto.
2. Authors, American—20th century—Biography.
3. Hispanic American gays—Biography.
4. Mexican American gays—Biography.
5. Gay men—Biography.
I. Title.   II. Series: Living out.
PS3557.O4695Z46   2013
813′.54—dc23
2012032924

for my nieces,
Halima, Annika Violet, & *Ga'aj Setareh*

for my nephew,
André

for my godson,
Pablo Ricardo

bless the smallest biggest joys

contents

|*contents*

II   unsettled independence

III   in search of paradise

IV   body cravings

acknowledgments

I gratefully acknowledge the editors of the following publications in which these works first appeared.

The Bloomsbury Review: "pseudonym"
Brevity: "sketch"
The Cimarron Review: "potato"
Green Over Katchina: "kill"
Hamilton Stone Review: "outcast"
Huizache: "crooked," "fire," "juguete," "lift," and
    "witch"
Many Mountains Moving: "clown," "insomnia," "rain,"
    and "voracious"
Pilgrimage: "biology" and "empty"
The Portable Boog Reader 3: "bleed"
Río Grande Review: "ghosts"
Urhalpool (online): "invisible" and "martini"
xQsí (online): "dream," "glove," and "papi"

A number of these pieces have also appeared, in slightly different versions, in the following anthologies: *The Moment* (New York: HarperPerennial, 2011), edited by Meghan Smith; *From Macho to Mariposa: New Gay Latino Fiction* (Maple Shade, NJ: Lethe Press/ Tincture, 2011), edited by Charles Rice-González and Charlie Vásquez; *Water's Edge* (St. Paul,

MN: Open to Interpretation Series, 2012), edited by Douglas Beasley and Anastasia Faunce; *The Rose Metal Press Field Guide to Writing Flash Nonfiction* (Brookline, MA: Rose Metal Press, 2012), edited by Dinty Moore; *Best Gay Stories* (Maple Shade, NJ: Lethe Books, 2012), edited by Peter Dubé.

Thank you to María Meléndez, for your sharp and sensitive editorial eye. Thank you to Rick Barot, for encouraging me to find a home for this book. And much gratitude to the Corporation of Yaddo, for that timely one-month residency in the summer of 2011.

autobiography of my hungers

allegory

like many Mexican children, I cleaned the *piedritas* out of the uncooked beans before they went into the pot — my meal-prep duty to help my overwhelmed mother as she spun around in the kitchen. The process was simple, but time-consuming: a pile of beans was placed at the edge of the table, I'd hold a bowl just below the edge to drop in the clean pieces, and I'd pick off the debris — dried-up seeds, miniature twigs, tiny stones — all of the undesirable, inedible stowaways. These would be set aside in a pile of their own, to be tossed at the conclusion of the cleaning.

I refused to dispense with my pile of detritus too soon since these were the fruits of my labor, the nuggets mined out of the sack. They were much more interesting than the beans, which huddled in the bowl, boring as clones.

I enjoyed holding up the small stones, especially, admiring the complexity of each shape, its many sharp corners, and the dark beauty of its coat gleaming with the light. If I pressed my thumb and pointing finger together, the stone would vanish, but I could still feel it, embedded there inside my flesh. So small a thing, but it had texture and strength. And sound. When I flicked it on the Formica table it tapped a rhythm the entire way until it leaped off the edge, delighted, it seemed, by its luck, its freedom, and its soloist song.

I

leaving the motherland,
mother leaving me

duty

for the households without washing machines, the place to do the laundry by hand in Zacapu, Michoacán, was at La Zarcita, the lake on the other side of town. My father carried the basket of clothes on his shoulder; my mother held my hand as we made the journey to the concrete washboards. We were still only three in that family, but my mother was pregnant.

Since this was women's work, my father took me to the part of the lake where young people swam. I squatted at the edge, making the surface of the water ripple with the tip of a twig. I forgot all about my father standing at a distance, he too lost in thought as he looked at my mother kneeling at the washboard, a white mass of suds expanding around her. They were in their early twenties, chained to domestic responsibilities and anxious about money. But I didn't know this yet. I only knew that they were all mine.

An empty bag of laundry detergent floated in front of me, its plastic body bloated with air, so I snagged it with the twig. One more game: I tried to fill it with water. But when I leaned forward I fell into the lake. My father and the sound of the women washing disappeared.

When my father pulled me out, I was too stunned to cry or complain as I stood naked in the sun, my shirt, shorts, and socks splayed out on rock. I had seen this sight the night before: a tinier version of my clothing stretched across my mother's lap, which was too crowded to sit on. I prayed my father, shaking his head at my stupidity, didn't make the wish I had made last night: for the clothes never to be filled with flesh.

piedrita

I find my little brother's baby sweater   in the bottom drawer and something
compels me to try it on   though even my little brother has long
outgrown it.
His shoes look like odd tiny cubes so I don't even bother.
But his pacifier,   plucked right out of his mouth, fits
into my mouth just   perfectly. Now, how to climb into the crib.
How to squeeze
his plump body   through the narrow wooden bars.

potato

the "apples of the earth," they're called in France, and in Spain, "patatas"; but in the Spanish-speaking Americas we call them "papas," from the Quechua, and they always sit at the center of the table, silent witnesses to the meals that we have or don't have in our crowded homes.

When I was a child I marveled at the versatility of this vegetable, how it was like a stone but could not break glass, how it was like an apple or a pear but without the sweetness, how it could calm our appetite but could not do away with hunger, which always came back, looking for its empty chair in our dining room.

Yet the potato was always with us, our angel from the ground, our missing piece to the cavity of the hand, the mouth, and the stomach.

I woke up in the middle of the night with a pain in my belly and I stepped off my bed with a mission: I would wake my mother and ask her to fry me a potato—only the sound of the skillet, only the smell of the oil, would comfort me. No, we were not going to starve, despite what Abuelo had said the week before.

As I made my way through the living room, I caught sight of the basket of potatoes on the table: each tiny head asleep and plump with meat. It was like sneaking into the chicken coop and finding the chicks huddled against the hen. But here there was no hen. We had eaten her. *How foolish*, I thought. *We will never again have eggs.*

zacapu

In Purépecha, the town's name means "rock," though we have been chipping away at it for generations, flattening the landscape and replacing the boulders with brick.

The Purépecha are my paternal grandmother's people. Short and dark, like many of us, they come down from the mountains to sell chapatas and nopales. They do not please the bank tellers when they walk through the doors in dusty sandals and rebozos cradling crying babies.

Purépecha songs are called *pirekuas*. Festive but sometimes melancholy, they are crooned with guitar, and late at night when Abuela thinks everyone's asleep.

"I want to learn more Purépecha," I said to Abuela as I put my head to her breast; she had just taught me to say tortilla—*chúscuta*. But then Abuelo burst in: "Don't be stupid. You'll have to learn English where *you're* going."

I bit down on the words to keep them in my mouth a little longer: *Purépecha, chúscuta, pirekua, Zacapu*. The afternoon light dissolved into the evening like salt in the bowl of soup.

piedrita

English is an ugly language,   *my friends inform me, though*
      no one explains further. It is   *one more truth*
about the United States to accept at face value.   *Up there,*
      I will have to wear cowboy boots and
a black leather string instead of a tie.   *Up there,*
      I will marry a woman with long, yellow hair.
She will be pretty,
      but she will feed me tasteless hotdogs   *every day.*

juguete

i was allowed to take only three personal possessions to
El Norte. We would be traveling by bus for three days and
two nights, my mother, my brother, and I, to meet with my
father and grandparents at the U.S.–México border. My
mother packed our clothes. My brother made his selections
but he refused to show me — those three things were the only
things that were only his and he wanted to keep it that way. I
chose a green car, a Beetle that looked like a plastic honey-
dew melon; *The Little Drummer Boy*, a book with a gold spine;
and a toy soldier, the biggest among the smaller armies that
my cousins knocked down by rolling marbles across the
kitchen floor.

"Why are you taking this thing? It takes up too much
room," my mother said. The soldier poised with a pointed
rifle was a clunky *L* in my suitcase.

"Because," I said, "I want to impress those gringos. I bet
they've never seen anything like *this*."

My mother raised her eyebrows but packed the soldier,
and I would always remember him that way, snug among
my shirts and socks, resting his weapon all the way to another
country. I would come to understand his loneliness also
because once we settled into our California house, he got

tossed inside a box with a book and a miniature car for company—all three objects going cold next to the refrigerator when the electricity got cut off and the house didn't feel like home.

trash

We didn't have a washing machine at our house, so at week's end my task was to take the laundry down the street to my aunt's. My mother would walk over later in the afternoon to do the wash.

The clothes were packed tightly into a trash bag, which I balanced on the handle bars of my bike. Usually I didn't complain about the chore. I was ten, and the ride was an escape from our crowded little house with its squeaky stairs and broken refrigerator door. One time I made the trip reluctantly because of what I'd overheard the week before: "Every time there's less for that woman to wash," my aunt had said to her neighbor, "because their rags have more holes."

En route, I was distracted by the echo of the insult and by the truth that ours was the poorest branch of the family tree. So when I came upon a Dumpster, it seemed quite logical, mechanical even, that I drop the lumpy trash bag into its huge, square mouth. Dissatisfied with the quickness of the gesture, I rolled back around to empty the contents over the spoils of fly-infested waste.

How pleasantly surprised I was when I thought that my mother had decided finally to toss out our old clothing with all its embarrassments — tears, snags, and stains that never came off. And a second later, how devastated I was that I had deliberately thrown away the clothing we were going to have to wear next week. I stood on my toes at the edge of the Dumpster as I pulled at my shirts, my mother's bra, my father's pants, all the while dreading what else my aunt would have to say about our rotten smell, our additional layer of filth.

lift

It's not as if we didn't have elevators in México, but I had never used one. I simply passed by banks, hotels, office buildings on my way to the single-story market, bus station, school. But then, at ten years old, after migrating to California, after getting sent for a physical by the school nurse, there I stood in front of the tallest hospital I had ever seen.

While Abuelo drove around to park the truck, Abuela guided my brother and me through the sliding doors, to the counter to ask the receptionist for directions, to the large metal doors without doorknobs, its row of numbered buttons lighting up along the top like on the arcade game machines.

"When we get inside," Abuela said, "you have to hold on. We're going to be lifted to the doctor's office."

Immediately my body froze. I imagined a swift ride through the air, getting pulled out like the weeds that we toss over the fence to shrivel with the sun.

The doors opened, we stepped inside, and then we huddled to the back, our arms linking to the metal bar and to each other, until Abuela pushed the button and the heavy doors closed.

There we were bracing ourselves for liftoff, for travel to another building, I thought. And I resolved right then and there that the next time I played outside, when I saw one of those metal boxes passing by, I would stop, look up, and wave.

witch

My witch was a poor witch: no shoes, a black tattered dress with patches crawling over it like red and blue spiders, and a shaky black house with curtains on the window that matched her dress.

My witch was a sad witch: face unfed, hands the barren breadbaskets that sit at the center of the table with their mouths open, waiting for a crumb. She was certainly unique among the other witches that looked the same: ugly mole on the nose, green skin, and yellow eyes. But without exception each frightening witch sported a clean black dress, the buckles on her black shoes, on her black hat, shiny and polished and new, as if she had just taken her scaring dress out of its factory box. My witch was the only one drawn in profile, as if she couldn't look you in the eyes to ask: "Is there anything to eat?"

I stood at the front of the room to explain my witch's poverty and I couldn't come up with anything to say, except that things were looking better for this witch: she had migrated to the United States, she had a job and loved the secondhand stores, where everything was used, but nothing had holes and so there was no longer a need for patches.

"And is this your witch's name?" the teacher asked, pointing at the word I had printed at the bottom of the page.

And that's when I froze because I had written *Avelina*, my mother's name, the prettiest gift I could find to console this poor witch who had traveled so far just to discover that her broom was to sweep the gingerbread houses of all the other witches the kids had drawn for fifth grade Halloween.

piedrita

Walking into the grocery market . . . how cruel.
All that food we are not   going to consume.
After an hour of strolling,   dazed behind my mother
                    and that shopping cart with its see-through ribs,
I stand at the checkout   next to a temptation of candy.   I know
          better than to ask for any.   But I also know it will be
weeks before we are back again,   so I swipe a candy
                    and throw it in my mouth, tearing up
as I swallow it whole.   I leave the wrapper on, intentionally,
          thinking: It will last longer that way.

fire

i joined the excitement down the street, where crowds had gathered from a safe distance to witness the wall collapsing from the weight of the water spewing out of the fire truck's hose. The displaced family stood apart from the rest of us, like actors on the stage at the end of the play. Indeed with the front wall of the house gone, the living room became completely exposed, the blue couch and the television like props on a set.

When the firemen finally shut off the hose, the flames completely snuffed out, there was applause and the people of the household looked confused, as if they were unsure about whether or not they should go back inside and continue living their day-to-day activities, ignoring that transparent fourth wall. They had been crying all this time, their grief so public that I imagined there was nothing else they could do in front of the neighbors that would bring them shame.

I saw myself riding my bicycle the rest of the week, passing the house in the afternoons, and catching a glimpse of the mother picking at her hangnail on the couch, the potbellied father walking around with his shirt off and farting, and the daughters arguing and pulling at each other's hair. But no such luck. Yellow strips of plastic ribbon cut off the abandoned house from the rest of the neighborhood and the family was never seen again. I envied their exit as I mourned how the rest of us had to vanish into our homes each evening only to ascend the next morning with the same needs as the day before, no more interesting than yesterday.

x-mas

at the time of the photograph, I didn't notice the tree going hungry in the back, its plastic branches spaced apart like bones on a ribcage. The tinsel drooping like strings of saliva. An anemic rosary of Christmas lights. My brother and I knelt in front of the tree, our striped shirts compensating for the dearth of gifts beneath it.

I do remember how proud my father was that he had cut out the perfect star from a cereal box. He had wrapped it tightly in aluminum foil before he placed it at the tip of our skinny tree. It seemed like an ingenious solution back then.

My mother made us change our poses repeatedly as we held on to the same presents. And then my father got into the picture, and then my mother traded places with my father, and then I traded places with him, all of us pretending we were capturing a moment of joy on the most magical day of the year. All of us pretending that my mother wasn't sick, that my father hadn't wasted his paycheck with his drinking buddies once again.

"Just a few more," my mother informed us, and we pasted those false smiles back on our faces the way my father had stuck the fake star on the tree. We had to use up the entire roll of film because it was a borrowed camera. The neighbors wanted it back by the following morning, which was Christmas Day for everyone else.

crayon

Another birthday and no party. No presents, either, except for a dollar bill, if my father remembered not to spend all his money on beer. My aunt, taking pity on the emptiness of my day, asked me to come over to her house for a surprise. I bathed and wore my cleanest shirt, expecting a piñata in the shape of a boat, a cake on display like a blue visitor from another planet, all of my cousins envious because today I was the center of the circle of their bodies.

I walked into her house and the living room was motionless, my uncle asleep in front of the TV. I worried he'd be startled when my cousins jumped out to yell *Surprise!* When my aunt came out of the kitchen I became confused: she wasn't wearing her party dress, or even the nice white blouse she sometimes wore to the post office.

"Happy birthday," she said, simply, and handed me an old box of crayons. The week before, my cousins and I had been Dumpster diving and we had fished out a collection of these discards from the elementary school across the street. My aunt took one from my cousin's stash and gave it to me, the name *Michael* scribbled on the box with black marker.

"Tell your mami I'll call her later," she said by way of asking me to leave. I did. On the way home I tossed the box of crayons back into the trash where it belonged. Its rescue had been temporary and a waste of time.

note i

Mami, I wrote to my mother, *stop calling me fat. I will run away if you don't accept me like I am.* I placed the piece of paper on the nightstand, beneath the largest bottle of pills. She was bound to find it, she in bed most of the day, groaning with pain I didn't understand. All I knew was that her condition made her cranky and sometimes cruel, punishing me because my body resembled the one that was betraying her.

"It's her heart," my father informed me when I came home from school and she was gone to the hospital again. I took advantage of his grief and walked to the cupboard to grab the bread my mother had asked me not to touch.

I was just about to take the first bite when suddenly my father slapped it out of my hand. "You're too fat!" he yelled, his eyes red with rage.

When I went to toss the soiled piece of bread into the trash bin I saw my note, glowing as white as the walls of the hospital. Suddenly I was overcome with shame and began to wail.

To comfort me, my father offered me another slice of bread. I ate it, and then later that evening I devoured the entire loaf in the cover of dark to punish myself even more.

crooked

My mother had crooked teeth, my brother has crooked teeth, and so do I. Braces were not an option in a household where I had to break open my piggy bank one summer to help my mother pay for a crooked suitcase sold to us by a neighbor. Even then I knew our neighbor had let go of her luggage out of pity. We were going to visit México, where crooked things like sidewalks were commonplace. Unlike last winter's Christmas tree with the crooked branches hiding beneath anemic silver tinsel. At the base, cereal boxes recycled to hold Christmas presents—the wrapping couldn't hide the unevenness of the rectangles-turned-rhomboids. And neither could the spirit of the season disguise the sadness of my mother's illness. There she was, lying on the couch in her nightdress at three in the afternoon, bracing herself for the tough decision of flying back to the homeland because she could no longer care for the household.

So there we were, half a year later, at the airport, waiting to ride an airplane for the very first time, my mother holding a rosary. The cross had snapped off somehow, but she held the string tightly anyway. What did a little damage matter when we had come so far? My brother stood close to her, a bag of warped plastic dominoes in his backpack, and I sat on the crooked suitcase, the sediments of my broken piggy bank settling like cookie crumbs from a cookie I never bit into with my crooked teeth.

piedrita

My uncle, my mother's youngest brother,
         walks into the bedroom where I am   pretending to sleep. All day
I have been crying because my mother is gone,
and the weight of my relatives comforting me has   worn me out. Lying down
        with my eyes closed is the only way   to be left alone.
           When he reaches down to feel my stomach, I know
he is checking to see   if I am still alive.
              We have already lost my mother.

biology

My grandparents loved to work with soil and claimed for their exclusive use whatever small plot of land we were entitled to in our low-income housing in California. Abuela grew flowers, vegetables, and herbs; Abuelo, trees. By spring, our tiny yard was cluttered with roses, mint and tomato plants, fig, papaya, and lime trees.

Ours was the only home without a lawn to wander on, and I thought it was yet another way to suffocate a teenager, like the seven o'clock curfew, the rule against personal phone calls, the policy of no visitors allowed. I accepted my fate now that my mother had died and my father had remarried and moved away. Each week I became more timid with sunlight. And while everything flourished outside, I stayed indoors, where the only growth was the moss in the narrow crevices between the cinderblocks.

So it pained me then that in high school biology I got this assignment: insect collecting, identifying the genus and species of each specimen caught.

"Will you help me?" I dared ask my grandparents, they who ventured out into the natural world. Without a second thought, they joined my search.

I continued to be amazed: we reached the twenty-insect minimum without leaving the garden. The creature life—ant, pill bug, bee, wasp, centipede, black widow spider—was as abundant as the flora. We crawled among them, my new guardians and me, sifting through the rosebush, lifting pots and shaking trees, coaxing each little wonder into the big light.

wicked

Abuelo did his share of damage to our family before he died, but nothing as twisted as what he did to the neighbor, an elderly man who kept taking Abuelo's parking spot. I knew he was in for it when he answered Abuelo's complaint with a dismissive "You don't own it. It belongs to whoever parks there first!"

That night Abuelo slashed the old man's tires. Since we lived in a low-income housing project, the run-down car was doomed to sit there, useless and abandoned. By the end of the week, the old man, a retiree like Abuelo, walked everywhere, his elderly wife in tow, both of them hauling groceries on foot.

The old lady eventually collapsed from who knows what. The ambulance came to pick her up though it never brought her back. By this time the car had a warning sticker on the windshield—it would be towed by the end of the week. Abuelo, flaunting his own wheels, drove in and out of the projects with glee, passing the old man as he made his slow trek to the hospital, which was, mercifully, not far from where we lived.

And then one day, coming home from school, I noticed the old man had pulled up his own chair to sit outside our apartment. When I walked up to open the door, he said in a disoriented tone, "It's all gone now. Everything's gone."

The run-down car on Abuelo's parking spot had vanished. A few days later so did the old man. When a different elderly couple moved in next door, my body stiffened if I happened to look out the window as they drove past, looking for a place to park.

dream

for months after my mother's death I had a recurring dream: that I was riding an aerial tram as it slowly descended a mountain. I didn't see myself but I knew I was inside the metal gondola suspended on the cables. Nothing tragic ever happened, but the feeling of weightlessness, of stomach queasiness, woke me up stunned and frightened each time. At twelve years old, I didn't expect the nightmares.

I was not alone those nights. Since we had moved in with my grandparents, there were four of us in that room now: my unmarried uncle in the top bunk, my cousin in the lower one, and my brother and me sharing a bed, half of which had to sit length-wise into the closet so that all our furniture could fit. My brother and I took turns sleeping on the side beneath the hanging clothes.

On the nights I slept with the row of garments grazing my entire body, that's when the bad dreams came. Always the suffocation before sleep, always the anxiety of falling as the aerial tram glided down.

And then one night, the quick relief of waking up was not enough. I decided to cry out deliberately, hoping that someone would rush over to my rescue. But no one moved or even whispered from another bed, *It's fine now; it was all a bad dream*. My cousin, my brother, my uncle simply slept — or pretended to sleep — through my girlish episode.

I knew then that I had reason to be scared: if anything should happen to the tram, help would be slow in coming. Or never show up at all.

piedrita

Why does he always come back to visit?
Each time my father   *leaves, it is like losing him*
     all over again.   *I just want him to stay*
     away.

glove

My father bought me a left-handed baseball glove, which
made my hand look large and masculine, not the feminine,
delicate hand I had to remember not to press against my
hips. As soon as I slipped it on I knew I would be bored, and
I made no effort to hide it as he stood a few yards away, yelling
out "Catch!" as if I were made for this meaningless task. The
baseball flipped over my gloved hand each time, my wrist a
hinge.

I could see the frustration in my father's eyes as my cousins
stood around to watch, my uncles judging from a distance. It
would be yet another athletic failure. His first: the boxing
career that didn't work out. And I, his oldest, nothing of a jock
in my baby fat, my soft voice, my gentle nature. I collected
stamps and books. I held my girl cousin's hairpins while she
tightened her braids.

My mind wandered, and I changed the ball into an egg,
the red membranes glowing through. A seashell holding its
salty breath. An avocado pit turned bone-white in the desert
sun. Or maybe, just maybe, it was John Steinbeck's pearl. I
saw all of these wonders flying toward me, but not the baseball itself. The baseball, full of manly rage, came charging at
my chest, striking my sternum with a thud that yanked me

out of daydream and into the terrible world of disappointed fathers and uncles who willingly exchanged their spectator sport from catch to knock-him-down.

migra

"Why don't one of you join the border patrol when you grow up?" my father suggested one time as we were inching our way toward the international border by car. We had spent all week visiting our cousins who, after all the trouble of getting their green cards, fled most of the year back to México. This made my aunt furious because she had spent countless days standing in long, insufferable lines inside buildings that amplified every heel that knocked on the tile. "I can still hear the echoes at night," she would claim.

"What for?" my brother said. "The job looks boring."

Indeed, all those years of crossing back and forth had given us nothing memorable. It was always the same questions, the same replies, the same look of disinterest from the man (or woman) in the migra-green outfit.

"It might make things easier," my father said.

I thought he was being funny, since we knew plenty of people who had lived in fear of getting caught by immigration, our mother included. Many of our other relatives had been deported more than once. We despised la migra, just like Americans despise the IRS—because they were an inconvenience. But the most-hated border patrol officers were the Mexicans. Such traitors. Why would we want to join *that* group?

When we finally reached the inspection gate, my father flashed his green card; my brother and I held up our American birth certificates. The guard, a Mexican, barked at my father, "How long were you in México? What are you bringing back?"

And then, so unlike who he really was, my father stuttered his reply, his body twitching in the seat during this single moment of powerlessness.

II

unsettled independence

invisible

freshman year of college I lived on the third floor of the dorms, and though there was an elevator, it was always quicker to sprint up the flights of stairs. The only time the elevator was useful was when I hauled my laundry to the basement. Every other week that was my routine, the trip so familiar I counted my breaths to it. That was how I knew I had descended too far, that the elevator had plummeted past the basement, which I never knew was possible. The small light went out and I was stuck there, in the near-dark, dirty clothes in my arms, a handful of quarters heavy in my pocket.

I pressed the emergency button and nothing happened. I pressed every other button repeatedly, refusing to let this small space get smaller still by having panic set in. I even giggled at my bad luck, imagining the story I'd tell later at the cafeteria while my dorm mates aligned the orange trays of food on the tables. It would finally be *my* chance to say something interesting since all this time I had nothing much to contribute to the daily dose of jokes, anecdotes, complaints, and witty observations flung from one side to the other. All this time I had been the listener, adding the sound of my laugh to the all-consuming din. I had yet to command attention, yet to be visible.

Then the terrible thought: What if no one noticed I was missing? It would be business as usual in the cafeteria, with silverware clanging and drinks spilling without me because I was the most insignificant of witnesses. And all the while me inside that coffin, buried in an unmarked grave, weeping at the memory of *them*.

piedrita

Library lighting at midnight stings my eyes,
                    but I can't   stop   reading.
          This is my newest craving   and I can feed it.
Word-fat books,   magazines aplenty,   poetry
                              that fortifies the lining of my brain.
          It's all discoveries like the female body,   like
the exotic kitchens I'm visiting for the very first time—
                              sticky rice, duck sauce, curry.

tongue

My only girlfriend in college is a Chinese immigrant and when we tossed around in bed I told her we were all beans and rice, my Spanish seasoning her Mandarin. She would roll her eyes and kiss me. She said there was no need for a condom at the peak of her period and my semen mixed with her blood and we never made a baby, though my father wanted me to bring one home one day. But every single sweaty effort got wiped off our bodies and flushed down the toilet.

"Will you marry me?" I asked her more than once, imagining my family's joy at bringing a girl to them. Not a blonde and not American, not really, but a pretty, fair-skinned girl, nonetheless, just like my dear departed mother. Every time she answered my proposal with an emphatic "no."

"Is it our families?" I finally said in exasperation. "Is it because you can't speak with mine and I can't speak with yours?"

My girlfriend laughed. "You know why," she said, coyly.

I did know. It wasn't the tongues we had but the tongues we wanted. She needed a man's. And so did I.

insomnia

at first it took only two pills to knock me out. Weeks later, I doubled the dose, though I quickly rounded that figure to five. These were my graduate school days in California, though it wasn't the deadlines or the heavy reading that kept me awake; it was Abuela's phone call: the family was moving back to México. Twelve years after our migration north, the González clan had decided to return. And once they left I'd be alone in this country, a severed limb twitching.

I told her that I was not going back with them, that I wanted to finish my master's degree. *Six pills, seven.* I told her that I'd be okay, at twenty-two years of age; I was a grown-up now, financially independent. *Eight pills. Nine.*

I didn't tell her, however, that I was afraid of my hungry gay body.

I was afraid of the light in the mornings, and the birds chirping from the branches of the tree outside my window. I was afraid of the door, always insisting I fill its empty belly with the swoosh of my passing through. At night, how I envied those little white pills, never sliding down my throat alone. They were like my family, acting as a cluster, invading any room they entered. To eat and sleep and dream together offered such comfortable safety. And then there was me, the errant charge, the stray, the boy who got lost in the woods and who had to survive by adapting to his isolated habitat. *Do like the squirrels and the chipmunks*, he told himself, *and gather the acorns. It's going to be a long winter.*

note ii

an inked goodbye.

It was not the first time I had written a suicide note, though I was certain that someone else besides me was going to read this one. I had grown so thin that I vanished beneath the covers. Once, a one-night stand was surprised to find me there when he pulled the blankets in order to make the bed. "You're sick," he said, and I didn't know what he was referring to. Had I indeed become infected with HIV? Or was I determined to starve myself into nothing because I was convinced nobody could love me?

I walked barefoot up and down the streets at two in the morning and stayed up until five, writing poems about dying. Life was lonely and exhausting, I had concluded, and I was ready to leave it all behind, the way my mother had.

Two days later the note was still sitting on my desk, just another badly written draft of something I had no intention to complete. Two nights before I had cut my right wrist and had intended to bleed to death. But I awoke with my crusty hand stuck to my face. The smell was metallic. I tasted like a penny.

"You don't know what you are worth," the woman at the crisis center told me.

"But I do," I replied.

night shift

to supplement my income while going to school, I took a position as a residence counselor at a group home for developmentally disabled adults. Since I was new I was given the graveyard shift, working from 11:00 p.m. to 7:00 a.m., and all I had to do before I left was feed the residents breakfast and start dispensing pills. Otherwise the job was low maintenance. Most of them, knocked out on medication, slept all night. I slept a few hours at a time, slumped over the dispensary desk, playing music at low volume. I had taken up smoking because everyone around me smoked, and I sat on the back porch in front of a bucket all the other counselors also used as an ashtray.

One night, craving company, I ventured to have a smoke on the front porch, where a few night owls sat past midnight. No one even flinched when I took my place among them. We all puffed away in silence, four weary bodies breathing in each other's stale air.

Around one in the morning, a man walked by and stopped in front of the porch. "Good evening," he called out. "Isn't it past your bedtime? Shouldn't you all be inside?"

No one answered.

Frustrated, the man then asked, "Is your counselor around? Can I talk to him?"

After a few seconds of silence, one of the residents replied, "No one here but us crazies." The rest of us laughed. When the man stormed off, shaking his head, we laughed harder still as the cigarette box was passed around, and I couldn't remember if it belonged to one of the residents or if it was mine.

xóchitl

She was my cat, a stray calico that gave birth on my bed on the night I took her in. I gave the four kittens away as soon as they stopped their suckling, my poor Xóchitl nearly sucked dry. She didn't look for them once they were gone, and I knew she was my kind, unsentimental about moving on. To ensure that she didn't go through the ordeal again, I had her spayed. OVH—an ovariohysterectomy—the humane amputation of her reproductive system. She didn't seem to notice a difference and went about her day, licking her shaved belly until the stitches got absorbed by her fat. The scar, if there was to be one, would remain hidden when her fur grew back.

I envied her then, keeping her wound invisible. I would always be more explicit: my scar shiny on the forehead, my trembling lip when the phone rang and my boyfriend's little voice inside screwed two words into my brain: *It's over*.

Once I left my cat for a week, and so did the negligent cat-sitter, and Xóchitl never forgave me for her dehydration, for letting the litter box grow into a mound of lumpy shit. And once I fainted in the living room—an episode of hypoglycemia because, alone in this country, I had very little money to feed myself. Xóchitl stood over my face and waited, I was sure of it, for me to die so that she could eat me. I reached over to make her purr into my hands and this comforted me. I dragged myself off the floor. I didn't want to fault her for her instinct to survive. The thought of eating my companion had crossed my mind as well.

piedrita

I lost my appetite
        after my father died.
All these years later,   *nothing tastes the same.*

voice

My father's voice now slept in a box, in a recording I made as a joke the time I visited him on the border. My stepmother was in on it and baited him to say silly things, though silly things were what my father liked to say when he stood over a ditch, looking for toads on a mosquito-infested afternoon. I was slightly jealous of my half sister, who had asked for this unusual pet. I had seen my father play soccer goalie to her penalty kicks all day and I thought how unfair it was that she got to have the beaten-down father, the father too tired to stray or say no.

I haven't been able to listen to the recording since his death, and so his voice remains locked in a miniature cassette, much like his ashes remained in a small wooden box until the time came to toss the dust into that same ditch. I didn't want to hear my father's voice. What I wanted to recover instead was the image of my father as evening fell. How his body slowly darkened. How I loved him then, fading away from all of us standing around that time—his second wife, his daughter, the neighbors—and not only from me.

reprimand

dead now for decades, my mother. Yet I had been careful to preserve certain ceremonies in her honor: candles on her birth date (March 21), candles on her death date (September 12), candles on Mexican Mother's Day (May 10), and flowers for her grave when I visited Michoacán, where she's buried. Each time I came back, my brother asked me, though he knew the answer, "Did you take flowers to our mom?"

Since he had not returned to Michoacán, my brother didn't know how much the town had changed, and, despite the air of permanence, so had the cemetery. Every day people died, and so complete strangers transformed the familiar landscape of the graveyard. It was not so easy anymore to say, *To get to my mother's grave, walk up the left path, and two rows after the well, turn left. It's the tomb with the blue tiles.*

The last time I tried to follow my own directions, I became disoriented: the left path was disrupted by another grave, there was now a second well, another tomb was also covered with blue tile. When I told my brother this, he grew furious.

"How could you forget where she's buried?" he demanded. "How could you let her get lost like that?"

My mouth dropped, but I didn't respond. I didn't want to get in the way of my brother admonishing himself.

martini

dirty Absolut. Up. With olives. It was another way for me to feel sophisticated, a citizen unapologetic of his bourgeois tastes. Though in the back of my mind I knew that I would lose control by the second round and I would be no different than my father sitting in front of a twenty-four-pack of beer, the carton torn open and staring out with its gaping wound as can after can was pulled out, consumed. My father walked around shirtless, proud of his beer belly, his face swollen, shiny as a blister.

The more he drank, the more his handsome face disappeared. And I pitied him—widower, farmworker, drunk. How different I felt—college student, writer, social drinker—toasting my successes in the trendy city lounges where the cultured converged, all of us deceiving ourselves with accomplishment that we claimed mattered beyond our insular circles.

My educated friends, I concluded as I stumbled into a cab to flirt with the driver, must have learned from their fathers as well. I imagined each of them observing quietly in the yards of their childhoods, as the men joked and slurred and spat and congratulated themselves for how far they had come, for what better lives they had in America. Who could forget the beauty of a can of beer changing color as the day collapsed into the silence that grew deeper and longer? Who could blame us for our community of enablers, the blessed people who kept us from plummeting into the loneliness and despair of our anonymous everyday selves?

III

in search of paradise

station

the Mexican bus station bubbled with activity. Sitting down offered no respite because of the constant anxiety of noise that swarmed through the halls and polluted the air above the waiting rooms. That's where I found myself in Michoacán one summer, Abuela sitting next to me, her legs locked around her vinyl shopping bag as we waited for our bus to Zacapu. We had just returned from Mexico City, where my cousin helped me carry Abuela on and off the metro escalators, which terrified her. The bag followed us everywhere—to church, to the bakery, to the market, when, to our embarrassment, Abuela held her six-pack of beer inside her see-through bag, showing off her purchase all the way home.

When the gate was announced, Abuela insisted we stand first in line to secure our seats on the bus. And since we were early, she said, "I'll be right back. I need to use the restroom. Stand right here and *don't move the bag.*"

Ten minutes passed, then fifteen, then thirty. The line grew, the bus arrived, and Abuela had not come back. Discombobulated, I left the bag and went looking for her, asking a woman walking into the ladies' room to check for my grandmother. Nothing. Behind me, the people in line walked over Abuela's bag to climb on the bus. The bag sat there looking vulgar, mocking me with its stained Tupperware, unfinished needlepoint, and Abuela's soiled clothing, including her undergarments.

And then I saw a frail old woman looking confused, standing on a different line. Heavy tears ran down her cheeks, and when I got close enough I heard her wail, "*Somebody* stole my bag! *Somebody* stole my bag!"

piedrita

"You are just a tourist here," my brother says when I visit him
          across the border.   Not even the edge
of the country is my beloved   México—
         I hunger for the memory
               of what used to be,   but that means
that I'm the ghost here,   haunting the shadow,
               inhabiting the afterimage of an unpeopled eden.

kill

ᵐy brother's white rabbit ran free, its pulsing body fickle and erratic as it scurried in the backyard while my brother mixed cement. I stood next to the Great Dane, shooing flies off its face, wondering why the dog let the pests have their way.

Animals had always been my brother's weakness. He took my Xóchitl because he knew I wasn't kind to it the way people should be—never leaving pets alone for longer than a day, never throwing a shoe at them when arriving home with heat rash.

"Are you going to eat it?" I asked, pointing at the rabbit. He paused his shoveling and wiped the sweat off his brow. "Nah," he said. "It's fine the way it is."

And in the instant that we zeroed in on the topic, the rabbit hopped in front of the dog, which reacted immediately and locked its jaw around the white fur. The rabbit's red eyes faded away.

I laughed, finding humor in the rabbit's reversal of fortune. Just as I had imagined it as food, it becomes it! I wanted to share this moment of levity with my brother, but I noticed his tears as he went over to pull the slab of skin away from the dog. He tapped the Great Dane's head in reprimand and then returned to his task. "I don't want the cement to dry," he declared, his back to me as he plunged the shovel into the gray slush.

outcast

as a homesick immigrant, I longed to mix in with my people whenever I returned to México. Once I was in Taxco, in the state of Guerrero, though my family was from Michoacán, so I made do on this visit as an interpreter at a writers' conference. My private time was only in the evenings, while the gringos were having dinner, socializing with each other and not speaking to the citizens of Taxco through me.

At dinnertime I sat at the town square near the church and soaked up the evening energy—children running, music blaring, vendors displaying their wares. It was Semana Santa, a week of daily festivals, and tonight was the ceremony of the virgin's pilgrimage. A statue dressed in silk was brought out of the church on a platform carried by four young women. They walked at the center of a procession through the square, out of the town, the followers illuminating the way with large candles.

I joined them, pretending I was one of them, a faithful, a Taxco native. We walked down the mountainside, through the dark dirt road that led to a nearby village. A chapel bell rang, the virgin was deposited inside the church, and then everyone simply blew out their candles and went home. This was their village.

It was not embarrassment I felt as I stumbled uncertainly in search of Taxco in the pitch dark, or even fear after I lost my way and wandered the dirt roads for another hour or so. When I finally caught sight of a streetlight on the main road I did not feel relief; I felt cast out of every paradise.

eye

i lost my eyesight in Oaxaca for three days. A type of cyst on the eyelid I had been ignoring for months finally caught up with me, and so I had emergency surgery just hours after arriving by plane. The necessary blindfold after the removal of the cyst added to the injury—I'd be unable to devour the Oaxacan sights I had heard about for decades—though my sense of smell remained intact and I could appreciate the spices even if I couldn't see the artistry of the arrangement on the plate.

The textures made more mysterious the bites of food in my mouth but the flavors were dizzying and I realized then that the most important part had been taken away: that immediate pleasure of watching the meal being served. That initial excitement was very animal-like. Cats and dogs, goats and pigs: all responded with the same instinctual bliss at the impending moment of overcoming their hunger.

All I had was the sound of the loaded plate striking the surface of the table, the scent of the server's perfume, and sometimes the subtle hint of a temperature change on my face. I had been robbed of recognizing portion, of knowing ahead of time whether I'd go to bed with a satisfied belly, or whether I'd have to reach into the hotel drawer in the middle of the night for the granola bars I left sitting on top of the Bible.

kite

She chose México, she said, because she didn't feel ugly here, not like in the United States, she, a Persian girl fleeing the Iran-Iraq War with her family. We met in college in California, and after she graduated she flew south, perfecting her Spanish, teaching belly dancing to natives and tourists alike. Whenever I visited the homeland I stayed with her and we explored the sites—Cuernavaca, Distrito Federal, Texcoco. And that day, on a whim, we climbed on a bus simply because we liked the name of its destination: Papalote.

The town named Kite was an empty town, with a town square with bored street vendors, but the buildings looked modern and new as if the cement of their walls had just hardened. In the town of Kite there stood a beautiful church with a colorful display explaining the history of the piñata—the Italian seven-pointed star that symbolized the shattering of the seven deadly sins.

We sat on a bench, waiting for the next bus back to the city. We gave the peanut vendor our business and chatted beneath a festive string of *papel picado* over our heads. "How I miss my country," my friend declared. "How I miss mine," I replied.

Suddenly a small parade came through: six children dressed in costume, blaring trumpets as they danced around the square. And so it was appropriate, our presence there in a town empty of most of its people, many of them working in the North and sending money back to beautify Papalote because they were all expecting to return from exile. The trail of music guiding the way disappeared like smoke.

clown

On a visit to Coyoacán, I took a stroll through the plaza and came upon a crowd gathered around a street clown. Anything he did provoked a communal laughter—fake falling, scratching his head, dribbling water on his red clown shirt. I would have moved on quickly, unimpressed by the performer's antics, perhaps even embarrassed by the deficiency of his dress, by the poverty of the audience that didn't have to pay admission to see this clown in his homemade suspenders, a painted nose instead of a manufactured one, and a pair of old work boots, not the regulation oversized squeaky clown shoes. I would have gone about my afternoon, purchasing trinkets to take back with me to the United States, to decorate my wall with the colorful folk art of México. But then, from the kiosk, a little girl leaned over the railing, pointing and gushing and bouncing with her hands over her cheeks, so tickled by the unexpected gift of a clown outside a circus.

I remembered myself in that child, pleased by the simplicity of surprise: the ice-cream vendor ringing his bell around the corner, warm sweetbread fresh from the bakery, the canary escaped from its cage and fluttering around the living room.

How undesirable to grow up and move away when all the wonderful things are within reach: the candy dish, the television, mother and father.

The losses, the heartbreaks, the hungers—all the dark days have yet to come. Until then, the little girl will stand on her toes in the kiosk as if that will lift her voice above all others as she yells to the clown, "Behind you! It's behind you!" when he asks in his high-pitch voice, "Where did my little hat go?"

piedrita

Spain, Brazil, Scotland, Costa Rica, Switzerland
but I always come back to the first word—chúscuta—
                    imagine Abuela meeting Goya at the Prado,
strolling along the banks of Genève,   riding to the island of Itaparica
              by boat but longing for Pátzcuaro,   Nahuatzen,
a piece of goat cheese in her hand reminding her of home.

tether

the ocean along the coast of Brazil was deceptively calm.
And since it was clear and still as a swimming pool I decided
to swim laps, moving back and forth in the warm water. The
exercise was so effortless, so smooth, that when I lifted my
head from the surface again I discovered that all that time I
had been floating away. I was lost in the open sea.

Suddenly the sky darkened. Suddenly the ocean grew
opaque, and when I swallowed a mouthful of water in my
immediate panic it felt as if I had inhaled mud.

Death by drowning, I imagined, was going to hurt. I saw
my body filling up with water and swelling up like a weather
balloon, except that instead of a buoy my body would harden
into lead and sink to the ocean floor.

I surrendered to my fate, letting the tide carry me off
like litter, the drowned rat in the sewage pipe flushed out.
And in that stillness was the laughter of children playing on
the beach. How they had chuckled at my swimming trunks,
baggy and bulky. How they had stayed close to their mother,
a large and beautiful woman in pink, like a majestic creature
of the sea. How I had envied that safety, myself motherless
for decades, roaming the earth unwatched and unseen.

Or so I thought, until the miracle. Somehow I drifted like
wood back to the shore. When my toes touched the sand I

began to cry, returning to the ocean the salt that I had swallowed. I wasn't sure which mother had taken me in: my own, the one in pink, or Yemanjá, the great goddess of the ocean. Or maybe all three were one and the same.

papi

another June of fatherlessness, childlessness, while the word, *father*, floated through the air like pollen, the fecundity of it birthing memories of Apá, Papi, forgivable and forgiven on his one special day. But on the other 364 he remained that shadow of a man, afterimage, ring of condensation on the counter that slowly vanished. Even through my thirties and into my forties I still felt like the boy he abandoned at thirteen. I attended baptisms and baby showers, skeptical of my friends who said they'd love their newborns forever. I knew better: Every child became difficult to love or love back.

"You were born so small, and hairy, and ugly," my father once told me, "that I felt sorry for you. And now you look too handsome to be from this family."

We were driving to the Mexican border, he to return to his second wife, who was pregnant again, me on a visit from college to see my brother, who was still childless after two years of marriage.

He no longer asked me about being single, or about having children. I was no longer part of the world he and my brother inhabited. I was a citizen of the unattached, the people who left no footprints after they died.

"I'm scared for your brother," my father confessed. "I don't understand what's taking so long. I want him to know the happiness of being a father. There's nothing more beautiful in this life than having a son."

And I thought, not just yet, beloved brother. Don't rush into the misery of becoming the disappointing parent of the disappointing child.

godiva

i was standing on the side of the road in Bonnyrigg, Scotland, waiting for the double-decker bus headed to Edinburgh, when I heard the clop-clop of a horse. On the horse was a beautiful young woman with long, golden hair, and I thought, how Godiva-like she was in her beige riding outfit.

When I stepped back to give her space she giggled and said, "Would you like a lift?"

I couldn't resist, though when my crotch pressed against her buttocks I couldn't control an erection. Maybe it was the rhythm of the horse, the memory of the bed dancing with the weight of two bodies colliding. Maybe it was the heat of the rubbing—body to body to animal body. We cast a single shadow on the ground and I wanted our bones to meld that way so that I'd have direction, always, and always a mode of transportation.

But Lady Godiva dropped me off at the next bus stop, where I crumbled like a discarded cape—the bat I found in my room the night before wedged to the crevice on the fireplace until the cleaning lady pried it out with the poker.

piedrita

Back in Purépecha country,
The neighbor's daughter has her eye on me.
her invitation to Janitzio—
in the center of Pátzcuaro lake, where women
with charales.
and I'll remember that taste
I take her brother's penis

pretending I like girls.
Bored, I accept
island
court the men
She feeds me salted fish
when, a few days later,

in my mouth.

IV

body cravings

love

On the first night we made love, we slipped into each other's arms on the living room floor. The gesture was impulsive, and after a few awkward bumps against the couch, the bookshelf, the wall, we squeezed our muscles together until we were a pile of sandbags, airtight and thick with pressure. Only our moans could squeak through.

"I'm so glad you found me," he said, though I meant to say it before him—declare him my savior and excuse myself from the burden of making the relationship work. But it was *his* apartment, so it was *his* task to guide me, eventually, to his bed.

"Is it too soon to say I love you?" he asked. And I said, "Maybe," though I was pleased he said it first, holding on to the order of things for future reference: *It was you who said it. It was you who asked me to move in with you.*

He didn't turn on the lights, and I followed blindly, until we reached the entrance to the bedroom. The bed opened up like a life boat, a pair of pillows for life preservers.

"Come," he said. He held my hand, and then the rest of me.

In the afterglow I was struck breathless by thoughts of the months ahead: reaching for him before he reached for me beneath the sheets at bedtime, waking up next to the man who might bring me breakfast in bed if I didn't get up before him to make the coffee and scramble the eggs. And if the waters got rough, I could always beat him to the exit.

empty

a year after moving to New York City, I was still incredibly lonely, though I had just moved in with my boyfriend, another writer. He worked long hours, and I, just out of graduate school and still unemployed, stayed home to read and write. We held hands during dinner each night, and afterward I vacated the apartment to explore the city while he did his own reading and writing alone. By the time I came back home, he was already asleep, and I crawled under the sheets, trying not to touch him, knowing that two people whose paths rarely crossed would eventually miss each other completely.

I was walking alone one afternoon, anonymous and silent through the bustling city streets, stimulated by the speed of other bodies. I cut through the traffic and sat on a bench at Central Park. This is how I met him, the widower, the businessman from Thailand.

We met every night that week, the length of his stay. We talked and laughed and kept each other company. Once we went to the movies. And twice we shared a meal and a bottle of wine. Each time at the conclusion of our date we simply shook hands.

On our final good-bye, he cried because he was returning to his country, a land full of memories of his dead wife. I kissed his cheek and told him with a shaky voice that I under-stood. I knew what it was like to enter uninhabited rooms, to long for a lover and lie down with a ghost.

piedrita

Purple elephants on Lexington Avenue. I keep walking
toward them and expect them to vanish.
                    They don't.   I want to climb them
and lumber off the edge of Manhattan. I want to return
            to my country or theirs.   The keening—
                    is it me, turning the key to my lover's door?
Is it them, trapped in the seams with a million
                            Styrofoam tears?

sketch

İ noticed the guy sketching even before I sat down, but it was not a strategic decision at all. When I have a choice I sit facing the eye candy, and this guy was not even close to handsome. But it was the only available chair in the coffee shop, so I ended up facing the sketcher, who kept to his task throughout my stay. I sipped my cappuccino, read a few chapters of a novel, scribbled in my notebook—the usual New York City java house pastimes that allowed me to tune out the surrounding noise.

And then I got the "feeling." It was that intuitive feeling that someone was looking at me, checking me out. I looked up and the sketcher looked down at his drawing. I looked away. That feeling again. I looked up, and once again the sketcher looked down. Yes, the sketcher was checking me out, which didn't flatter me, he so plain and unattractive.

I looked down again. From the corner of my eye I saw him look up. He was using me as a model. I became uneasy, self-conscious about what unflattering version of me the charcoal brought out. So I left soon after, making believe I had my fill of the coffeehouse vibe. I went about my day, expecting never to see him again.

The following week I saw the sketcher, his sketches on display along the wall near the Union Square subway. And sure enough there I was, on sale for $5. I stood in front of it, expecting to be recognized, but no one did. In fact, I hardly recognized myself, looking so forlorn as if I were the forgotten mug, its smell of coffee going faint, its ceramic body growing cold, its handle longing for touch.

rain

One evening I got caught in a legendary Manhattan monsoon, and I bemoaned the drenching of my Kenneth Cole dress shirt, my black slimming slacks, my Italian leather shoes. The umbrella was useless, since the rains struck sideways as if from a fireman's hose, so I tossed it into a puddle and watched the spokes glare with the streetlights.

Then, the memory flash: Abuela, worried that we'd get caught in the rain and get colds, draped thick, plastic sacks over my brother and me after piercing holes for our heads and arms. I was ten, my brother eight, and we arrived at school looking like stuffed sausages. The kids laughed but the teacher didn't, sending a note home with me telling Abuela how dangerous this was, that we could have suffocated.

Abuela was indignant when I translated the note to her out loud.

And I remembered the time she bought a coconut cake for my birthday at the local market. The cashier had quipped under her breath, "Who would buy a cake like *this?*"

More memory: in junior high, Abuela asked my brother and me to wear the same clothing two days in a row. I didn't question the motivation, and to please her even more I'd wear the same outfit three days in a row, sometimes four, until a cruel kid walked up to me and said, "Did you know that people call you the Photograph?"

I feel liberated suddenly, the indignities of times past washing over me, draining into the sewage pipes beneath the New York City sidewalks. I let it all go — the sweat, the tears, and even the piss — every shameful fluid safely camouflaged by the cleansing waters of a stormy night.

chi

My lover and I rode the 6 train to Manhattan's China-town. It was our weekly excursion, this search for ingredients prominent in Asian cooking, and with it, always the wonderful assault of jade and calligraphy, fish and lotus seed, Mandarin and Cantonese. No surprise then to be intrigued by a Chinese fortuneteller speaking through a translator to a Dominican woman. The translator seized on my interest and grabbed my arm. I in turn convinced my partner to join in the fun.

The Chinese fortuneteller consulted his charts, my partner's hands and forehead, and had nothing but glowing things to report: "You are very intelligent. You will live a long life. You will have much luck if you wear a silver ring in your right middle finger."

I rolled my eyes at the generic prognostication, but humored the sidewalk encounter by taking my turn on the chair. "You will live a long life," the fortuneteller declared, "if you do not kill yourself."

Startled, I withdrew my hand. My partner turned pale, as if he has just been told what I've been withholding from him all this time. *So this explains it*, his face read.

I wanted to accuse the translator of mistranslating. Perhaps the word was "overwork": *You will live a long life if you do not overwork yourself.*

"He's got it all wrong," I said to my partner later that night. But he turned his back to me, feigning sleep, pretending he didn't know that all those times I turned my back to him I was only making believe I was awake.

piedrita

The sheets stretch across the mattress
as if the bed doesn't want to be disturbed.　　I sit on the floor next to my suitcase,
　　both of us like pets ready　　to run out the door.
The window　　widens on the wall　　like another mouth wanting to be fed
and all it gets　　is what's leaking down from the moon.
　　I have been tricked like that before
　　　　　when light fills the room but stays empty,
when a body cancels out the body lying next to it and no one's left to say
　　"I'm sorry."
A shadow cuts through the window.　　　　I want to believe it's the man
　　I'm leaving.　　I want him to recognize that without me
he's famished,　　that only I can nourish him with　　the spoons
　　I'm taking with me—my dimple, my big toe, my thumb.
　　But then the paralyzing truth:　　I have no one left to feed.

ghosts

My brother told me he saw a ghost in the hallway last night, a boy wearing a baseball cap mouthing to himself as he leaned into the bookshelf as if trying to make out the words on the spines in the dark. It was 5:00 a.m., the time of night when he rises to piss, to lumber along the cold floor from his bedroom to the bathroom at the end of the hall. It was the only time he regretted not having slippers; it was the only time he remembered all about the icy concrete beneath his feet.

When he stumbled upon the boy, my brother shook out of his drowsiness, and it was his hands that felt clammy now. But the boy didn't realize he had been caught in the mischief— escaping his ghost-world to take a dip in the realm of the living. So my brother gave him the universal *psst!* (It was understood in both English and Spanish and in the language of the dead, apparently.) Startled, the boy snapped his neck to look at my brother, and then scurried into the darkness, vanishing through the wall at the end of the hall.

He told me this on the cell phone as his truck crawled across the border on his daily international commute from México to the United States. I listened to the honking of my homeland as I looked out my window in my eighth floor New York City apartment. I told him I believed. I was certain that a previous tenant had died in my place, that the spirit roamed the room in search of the comfort of its bed. We were both lost, my ghost and I, and therefore had been adequately matched across the dimensions, just like my brother and his ghost because they were insistent border crossers.

pseudonym

Mike asked if my name was really Mario. He asked before sex, though I told him my name was Rick. I was not Rigoberto. Rigoberto knew better than to get picked up by a stranger for pseudonymous sex.

The strangers I slept with were all named Mike, or John. They had all slept with Rick, not Rigoberto. Though this Mike wanted to sleep with Mario, Mario who didn't want to admit to his true name because he was an educated Latino who knew better than to let himself get picked up by a stranger for pseudonymous sex.

When they introduced themselves at the bar the first time they met, a cosmopolitan glowing like lava in Mike's martini glass, Rigoberto told Mike his name was Mario, not Rick. They didn't have sex or even kiss. Mario knew better.

The second time they met, Mario was weak. He had just broken up with his boyfriend whose name, interestingly enough, was John. He missed John's warmth, the hard touch of his fingers tapping against his spine. The stubble of his chin, the wetness of his neck, the scent of his chest—all of these were on Mike that night and they seduced Mario into letting down his guard. "My name is really Rick," he said, and they kissed and they had sex.

The next morning, I woke up in Mike's bed and it felt comfortable and familiar.

"What is your *real* name?" Mike asked again.

"Mario," I said.

"I knew it," Mike said. And he reached over to embrace me.

piedrita

Lincoln Center romance: a woman from the symphony,
          her violin a twin   of her naked back.
                    I had forgotten the artistry of the female form,
the music of her fingertips, the song   of her moan—
                    the nurturing impulse.
I go home to my lover   and teach him
          a similar lesson.

questions

"What do you write about?" he asked, and I answered, quite simplistically, "Life," offering the man I was going to sleep with that night a bouquet of yellow flowers instead of a handful of thorns had I admitted, more truthfully, "Death" or "Violence" or "Pain," as in the horrors that writers will inflict on people who ask for them.

"Will you read me a poem in bed?" he asked, and I knew the relationship was over long before it even had a chance to start. How could I bring one of my paper loves to bed and not ignore the less interesting body of flesh and coarse hair, with its unimaginative vocabulary and without metaphor? And suddenly I felt compelled to crawl back to my poetry, begging forgiveness for this infidelity, daring to please my scarred skin-sack of brittle bone when greater pleasures awaited me on beds as white and expansive as heaven.

"Are you listening to me?" he demanded, or I think that's what he said; I wasn't sure anymore, and I didn't care anyway because I had put my clothes back on and was headed out the door, mumbling to myself, "I'm sorry. Will you forgive me?" and I knew I had made the right choice to leave because this idiot behind me thought that I was begging his pardon when he answered, "Of course, my darling. Call me."

note iii

i had to walk with a cane. Inexplicably I lost my balance and the doctors had yet to diagnose me with my affliction, but this didn't stop me from taking my strolls along the park.

I came across two young men practicing the tightrope and it nearly brought tears to my eyes, the unfairness of it all: how some people could steady themselves on a string while others must fear falling while walking on three legs over level ground.

The next Saturday, I came across the tightrope walkers again. There were three of them this time. And I limped up close enough to marvel at the miracle of balance. They noticed me and halted their act. I noticed the pity in their eyes, a glassiness bordering on shame. So I moved along.

One week later, we met again. The group had grown and by now we all knew that our schedules coincided: me on my cane, they on their rope. But out of some sense of politeness they ceased their fun long enough to watch me pass them by.

I was determined, the next time I saw them, to let them know there was no disrespect in their hobby. That when I cried in front of them it was an appreciation of beauty, not an expression of grief for my loss. But I never had the chance. The next week I came across a note on the trees that used to hold the rope up: *The funambulism club has moved! Call Darren for new location.*

piedrita

> *I am only able to walk in the mornings, and every morning*
> *I pretend there's nothing wrong with me,*   *there is no*
>   *cane propped up against the wall*   *waiting*
> *like a dog*   *for its afternoon stroll,*
>   *there is no*   *mystery illness—*
>   *a boa swallowing my body whole.*

haughty

i had always been something of a dandy: Ted Baker ties, Italian leather shoes, designer coats with epaulettes and buttons shiny as doubloons—all the prettiness that hid my impoverished past. But when I had to sport a cane I resented the accessory that had been forced on me. For years I had clenched my teeth at the old people slowing me down, rolled my eyes at their sudden loss of direction or disorientation, curbside indecision, and sidewalk zigzags. And now, there I was, holding back the New York rush down the subway stairs. How unfair was the grumbling and the griping, the teeth-sucking and sighing, my disability and limitations conspicuous and inconvenient to the two-footed species I was once a part of.

I went to Bloomingdale's one afternoon to pick up a pair of expensive black suede shoes and as I stepped out of the Third Avenue entrance I lost my balance and dropped to the ground. No one offered me a helping hand. I was not worth noticing suddenly, splayed out like a rug or a derelict or a spill of vomit going hard and odorless beneath the sun.

So I picked up my own bloody self, thank you very much, dusted my waistcoat, shook out my shopping bag, and hobbled to the nearest lounge for a martini, my cane resting its overworked backbone against the bar.

extraction

the second and third molars of my lower right jaw were impacted and had to be yanked out, finally, because one of them was turning black. I'd open my mouth and tongue the small blocks of enamel huddled together—a veritable pietà of bone.

I chose to remain awake during the extraction because I wanted to see the teeth stripped of gums. I imagined the oral surgeon plucking one out, then the other, with tweezers and placing them like a pair of beetles on a porcelain dish. I would take them home and make a necklace of the one that looked like a chip of obsidian arrowhead—an Aztec relic— for luck. But what I got instead was a doctor in comic goggles, a drill, and the cracking of quarry stone—a tin dish of breakage. The stitching, the tying of a shoelace. How everyday the procedure, how ordinary the numbness and subsequent pain.

The next morning I claimed my moment of originality, stubbornly, when I sneezed at my desk and spat out the stitches clutching to a piece of gum that landed on the computer screen like fish bait. The drops of blood splattered like on a television crime scene and the keyboard blurred like an X-ray of my skeletal teeth.

"That's a new one," the receptionist said when I wrote out an explanation on a piece of paper, my mouth stuffed with reddening gauze.

bleed

I've dressed my studio in red: red sheets, red couches, red desk chair. But it's the red hummingbird among a bed of roses on the monoprint that hurts the most. It's pinned to the wall like a gash slowly clotting.

I once cut my finger slicing into a bar of cheese, and I licked the blood drops on the counter because I was tired of the screeching of roses — how they kept me up at night, demanding comfort. No matter how long I pressed my tongue against the paper I only managed to reopen the wound of the hummingbird's wings.

My lover slept beneath the covers while I wrote, and I invented a name for him in the story about a man (who's a writer) who was going leave his lover because he didn't like the color of his lover's nipples — the stains of blood that wouldn't soften or come off the skin no matter how much, no matter how long he lapped at the nubs of red flesh.

To satisfy his lust for the erasure of red, he sat at his desk drinking glass after glass of merlot. Once he finished the bottle, he turned off the lights and made everything red disappear at once. But his lover's nipples, how they glowed like the tips of matches holding in their fiery breaths, how they radiated with the need for attention.

The writer in my story bit into his lover's chest, and the lover awakened to an hour of passion in bed. The writer in the room let his lover sleep. He bit into the swollen rose going dry inside the passionless bed of his mouth.

voracious

the refrigerator remained empty year-round. I was unable to put any food inside without pulling it out an hour later and consuming it all. It was the same for any perishable item: bag of chips, box of granola bars, a banana bunch. Not all at one sitting, but at thirty-minute intervals. I made frequent trips to the kitchen as if I were afraid the food would disappear, that some phantom thief would sneak into the building to satiate his appetite behind my back, that he would mock me because I was sitting so peacefully at my desk, confident that there was something in the cupboards the next time my stomach grumbled.

If the kitchen was bare there was no reason to walk into it, and no negotiation or exchange, no dilemmas about what to eat. I learned that in my mother's anorexic kitchen the days I was allowed to lick her hands clean when I wanted seconds; I learned that in Abuelo's stingy kitchen the days our meals were rationed.

I was dining with a friend at a fancy eatery in Brooklyn. The food arrived. A modest portion, it was garnished with rosemary and a beet carved like a swan. A thick red sauce swallowed every curve and angle touching the surface on the dish. To my date it was a work of art. To me it was the Mardi Gras mask worn by the yellow skull of famine.

Hunger was one of the ghosts that still haunted me, the anxiety that forced me to clean my plate at each meal. It had been decades since the last time I'd had to confront my jaw twitching around an empty mouth, the tongue going dry and stinking like fishbone. But the fear of starvation stood next to me always. He was the little boy with long cheeks, and a pair of eyes like dead stars that ate up the light.

piedrita

I say, I want to live, and my doctor says, yes,
    you should,   and you will
           if you stop getting so depressed about the things
that happened so long ago   no one else but you
          remembers them.   I say, What I do is better—
I write them down on paper,   each sad memory like
          a headstone in a cemetery where nothing remains buried—
isn't that a kind of living   with so many dead things
     walking about outside their coffins?   Should I stop
      and let everyone back in their graves?
     Until you do, my doctor says, there's no chance
             of forgetting.   I say, no,
               I can't live   with that.

forest

While traveling in Switzerland I went on a walk among the vineyards and the apple orchards, picking at the fruit and marveling at the size of the sunflowers lounging at the side of the road like a pride of lions. From across the field I spotted her—an old woman dressed completely in black, a storybook witch on her way back to the forest.

Since I was seeking adventure on this otherwise quiet expedition, I followed her into the dark and silent woods, and I cursed my curiosity for taking me there. Until I stumbled upon the gingerbread house. It was actually a bird feeder hanging from a branch. And near the trunk was a chair made to look like a horse: a bucket shaped the mouth; dried leaves made the perfect ears. More transformations: plastic soda bottles became a mobile of airplanes; cans were crushed into mushrooms; an old boot opened its miniature hippopotamus mouth.

But no sighting of the artist. The old woman had done this, I was certain, so I respected her work and vanished, leaving her dazzling forest museum unmentioned, unphotographed, and for many years, unwritten, until I saw her figure reappear in my mirror at home, hunched over a cane, clad completely in black, and gathering bits and pieces of this and that in order to build a gallery of tiny gems, colorful and edible as gumdrops.

LIVING OUT

Gay and Lesbian Autobiographies

David Bergman, Joan Larkin, and Raphael Kadushin
SERIES EDITORS

The Other Mother: A Lesbian's Fight for Her Daughter
Nancy Abrams

An Underground Life: Memoirs of a Gay Jew in Nazi Berlin
Gad Beck

Gay American Autobiography: Writings from Whitman to Sedaris
Edited by David Bergman

Surviving Madness: A Therapist's Own Story
Betty Berzon

You're Not from Around Here, Are You?
A Lesbian in Small-Town America
Louise A. Blum

Just Married: Gay Marriage and the Expansion of Human Rights
Kevin Bourassa and Joe Varnell